T0400468

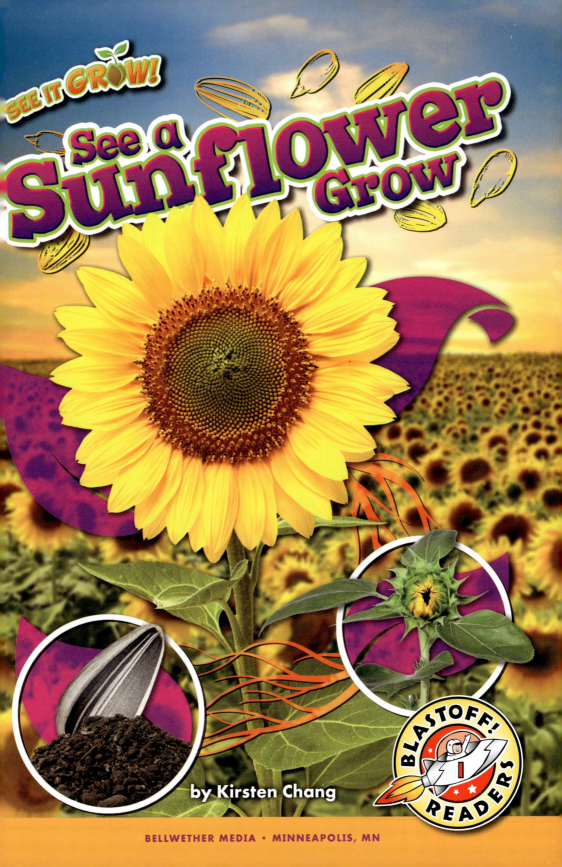

SEE IT GROW!

See a Sunflower Grow

by Kirsten Chang

BLASTOFF! READERS

BELLWETHER MEDIA • MINNEAPOLIS, MN

Blastoff! Readers are carefully developed by literacy experts to build reading stamina and move students toward fluency by combining standards-based content with developmentally appropriate text.

Level 1 provides the most support through repetition of high-frequency words, light text, predictable sentence patterns, and strong visual support.

Level 2 offers early readers a bit more challenge through varied sentences, increased text load, and text-supportive special features.

Level 3 advances early-fluent readers toward fluency through increased text load, less reliance on photos, advancing concepts, longer sentences, and more complex special features.

★ **Blastoff! Universe**

Reading Level

Grade K

Grades 1–3

Grade 4

This edition first published in 2023 by Bellwether Media, Inc.

No part of this publication may be reproduced in whole or in part without written permission of the publisher. For information regarding permission, write to Bellwether Media, Inc., Attention: Permissions Department, 6012 Blue Circle Drive, Minnetonka, MN 55343.

Library of Congress Cataloging-in-Publication Data

LC record for See a Sunflower Grow available at http://lccn.loc.gov/2022039506

Editor: Betsy Rathburn   Designer: Brittany McIntosh

Printed in the United States of America, North Mankato, MN.

Table of Contents

Flower Fields

Sunflowers are beautiful flowers! They often grow in fields.

How Do They Grow?

Sunflowers grow from small, black seeds. The seeds are planted in **rich** soil.

seed

The seeds grow roots. **Seedlings** grow out of the ground.

seedlings

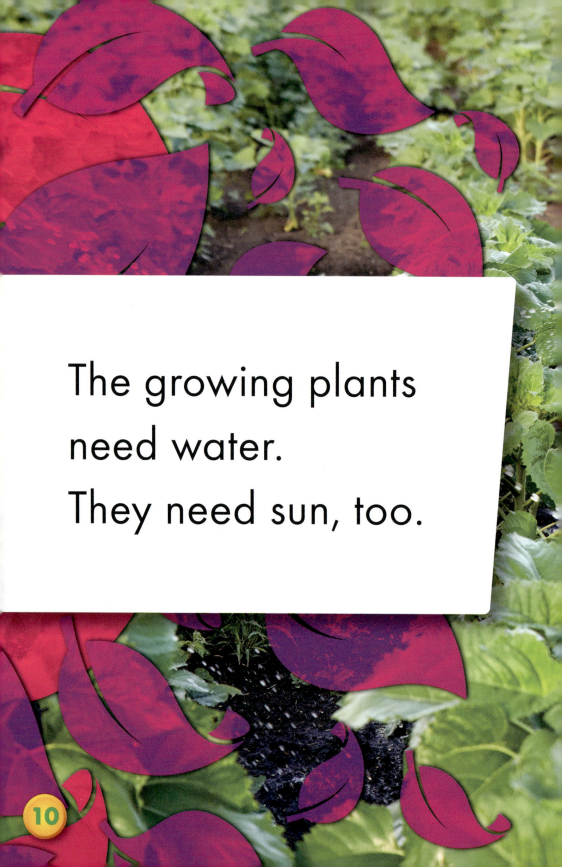

The growing plants
need water.
They need sun, too.

Needed to Grow

rich soil

water

sun

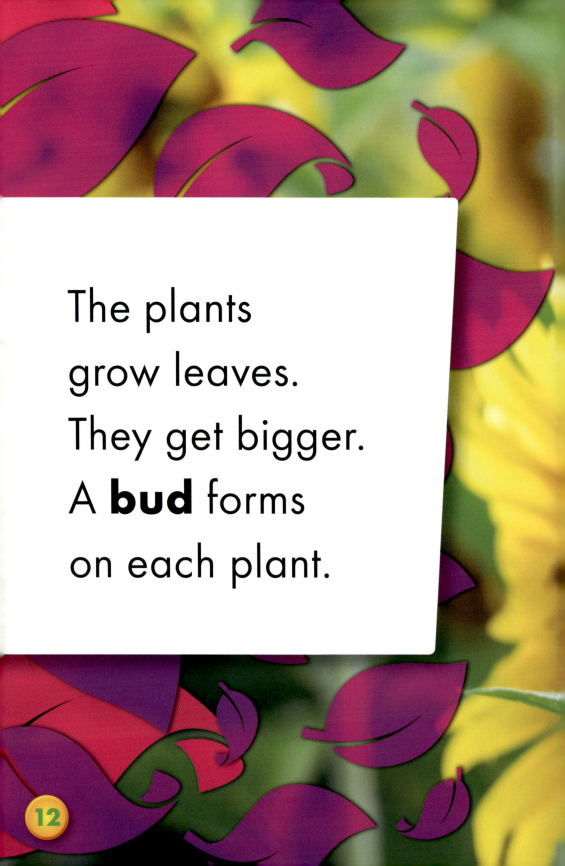

The plants
grow leaves.
They get bigger.
A **bud** forms
on each plant.

bud

The bud **blooms** into a flower. Bees **pollinate** the flower. Seeds form!

Fully Grown

Sunflowers can grow very tall. They can be taller than a person!

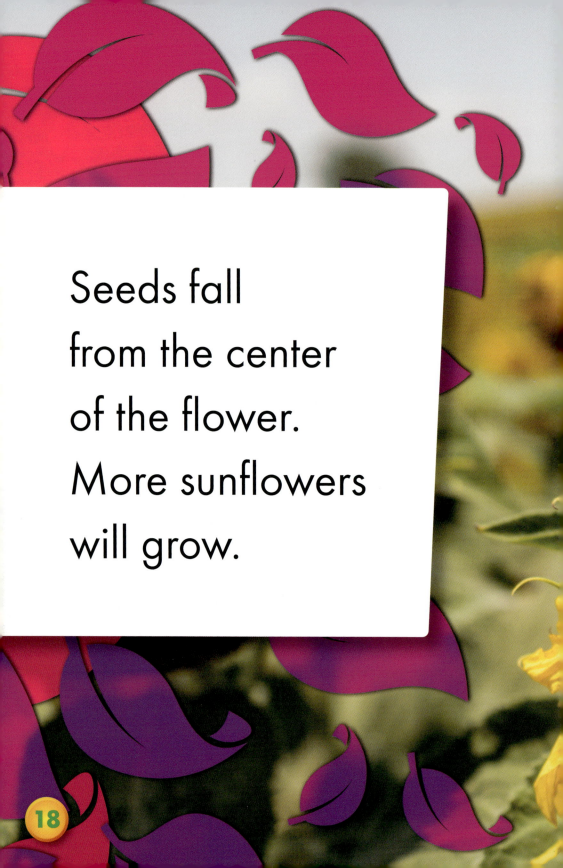

Seeds fall
from the center
of the flower.
More sunflowers
will grow.

Sunflower Life Cycle

1 sunflower seed is planted

2 seedling grows leaves and a bud

3 bud blooms and bees pollinate it

4 seeds form on the flower

seeds

Sunflowers can be cut for **bouquets**. We can eat the yummy seeds!

Using Sunflowers

bouquets

sunflower seeds

cooking oil

bouquet

Glossary

blooms

opens into a flower

pollinate

to give pollen to make seeds grow

bouquets

groupings of cut flowers

rich

full of the things plants need to grow

bud

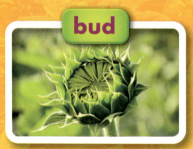

a growth that turns into a flower

seedlings

small, young plants

To Learn More

AT THE LIBRARY

Connors, Kathleen. *How Do Sunflowers Grow?* New York, N.Y.: Gareth Stevens Publishing, 2021.

Herrington, Lisa M. *Seed to Sunflower.* New York, N.Y.: Scholastic, 2021.

Sterling, Charlie W. *Sunflower.* Minneapolis, Minn.: Jump!, 2023.

ON THE WEB

FACTSURFER

Factsurfer.com gives you a safe, fun way to find more information.

1. Go to www.factsurfer.com.

2. Enter "see a sunflower grow" into the search box and click 🔍.

3. Select your book cover to see a list of related content.

Index